D is for Doufu

An Alphabet Book of Chinese Culture

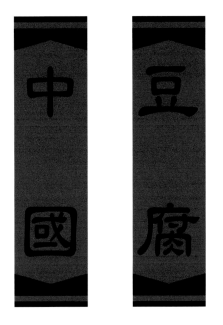

by Maywan Shen Krach
illustrated by Hongbin Zhang

Shen's Books
Arcadia, California

Author's Note

Among the many pictographic languages, including Egyptian hieroglyphs, only the Chinese written language has survived the evolution of pictographic words. Today it has become the most prevalent non-alphabet language in the world.

This book will illustrate the pride and joy one has in being Chinese by sharing the beauty and richness of the Chinese language and culture. For the student of Chinese, this book of personal reflections will rekindle and deepen ties to Chinese tradition. Many of the words in this book have been borrowed and shared by other groups. You may be surprised to find a little trace of Chinese in everyone!

When Chinese is written in the western alphabet, it is romanized. *Hànyǔ Pīnyīn* is the form of romanization used for each Chinese key word. Traditional Chinese characters and their English meanings are written next to them. The book introduces only 23 terms because there are no words that start with the i, u, or v sound in *pǔtōnghuà*, which Westerners know as Mandarin.

For my mother who taught me that simplicity is beauty
- M.S.K. -
For my daughter
- H.B.Z. -

Library of Congress Cataloging-in-Publication Data

Krach, Maywan Shen, 1953-
D is for Doufu : an alphabet book of Chinese culture / by Maywan Shen Krach ; illustrated by Hongbin Zhang.
[32p.] 30 cm.
Summary: An alphabet book approach exploring the beauty and richness of the Chinese culture.
ISBN 1-885008-06-6
1. China -- Civilization -- Juvenile literature. [1. China -- Civilization.] I. Zhang, Hongbin, ill. II. Title.
DS721.K73   1997   951—dc21   96-52163   CIP   AC

History of the Chinese Language

Written Language: Image and Meaning

It is believed that more than 3,000 years ago, an official imperial recorder in China observed the forms of nature and copied their shapes onto smoothed bamboo. Thus came to be the first Chinese pictograms. As time went by, these primitive drawings were stylized. With the increasing complexity and sophistication of the civilization, a need arose for Chinese characters that could express more than physical things. Symbols for emotional and intellectual concepts called ideograms were developed, and numerous words were invented.

Today, as the world evolves, new ideas and concepts are created and the Chinese written language continues to grow. New characters are made for new events and objects. In the process many old words have become obsolete. A typical Chinese 12-year-old knows about 3,000 characters. Between 4,000 and 6,000 are needed for fluent reading, and a highly educated Chinese may be able to use 10,000 characters or more.

Spoken Language: Sound

No matter how a Chinese character is constructed, each symbol stands for one sound. Since many characters sound alike, tones are added to distinguish them. This is why Chinese has a musical quality.

There are many ways to say a Chinese word. It all depends on which geographical area one comes from. This is called dialect. Sometimes dialects can be very similar and understandable from village to village; but most of the time, they are not. A Chinese word may sound different to different people, but it looks the same to everyone. Chinese people all over the world can communicate with each other and maintain their rich culture and language because there is only one written Chinese language.

There were so many distinct dialects in China, that it was difficult to do business. The Chinese government decided that Mandarin, which originated in northern China, should become the language in which all business would be conducted; but at home, people could speak their own dialects. Today Mandarin is the official dialect of both the People's Republic of China and Taiwan.

ài

love

In the center is the heart 心 . Above is breath 灬 and below is graceful movement 夊 . Love breathes life into the heart and brings grace to the body.

The Chinese believe that the human mind is in the center of the heart and that love comes from the heart. Love is a form of giving which should be extended not only to those closest to you but to more distant members of society as well. While it was once considered a highly spiritual emotion, today *ài* 愛 is used more freely to express affections.

To say one loves someone or something, another word must be added to *ài*; for example, *jìnài* 敬愛 for respectful love; *mǔài* 母愛 for motherly love; *qīnài* 親愛 for dear love; and *àiqíng* 愛情 for love between a man and a woman.

bǎi

jiā

xìng

one hundred surnames

Bǎi 百 represents one hundred. *Jiā* 家 means home. *Xìng* 姓 , the word for family name, is made up of the characters for woman 女 and birth 生 . Before the Zhou dynasty most Chinese family names had the symbol for "woman" in them.

The Book of Family Names, Bǎijiāxìng, is a classic primer for children in Chinese homes. Every child can recite the one hundred most popular surnames. According to a recent Chinese census, there are at least 3,730 one-character surnames and 2,630 multi-character surnames.

Every Chinese has great stories to tell about his ancestors no matter what surname he inherits. One third of the famous Changs in history were military figures. Lee, the most common surname, has been linked to countless political leaders — from the founder of the Tang dynasty to the contemporary chiefs of China, Singapore, and Taiwan.

chē

vehicle

Chē 車 is a bird's-eye view of a two-wheeled cart. The top and bottom lines 二 are the two wheels, and the middle box with a partition 甲 is the body. The vertical line | is the axle.

Legend has it that Emperor *Yǒuxíongshì* devised a peculiar push cart which he took to war. The cart always pointed south. This enabled the emperor's army to battle the guerrilla enemies hidden in the mountains without becoming lost. References to this extraordinary vehicle diminished during the Zhou dynasty when the compass was invented.

Chē can be added to other words to make new terms for different modes of transportation, for engines, and for machinery. A graphic example is *hōng* 轟 , the character for rumble or explode, which shows three cars involved in a pile-up!

dòu

fǔ

tofu

Beans and other vegetables with seeds in pods are called *dòu* 豆 . *Fǔ* 腐 is the process of fermentation.

Soybeans have long been a main source of protein for the Chinese. Soy sauce and *dòufǔ* are both popular products made from soybeans. *Dòufǔ* is sometimes called "Chinese cheese" by Westerners. Just as the Europeans ferment milk from animals and extract cheese from it, the Chinese ferment milk from soybeans to produce soft or hard *dòufǔ* for main dishes, soups, and snacks.

People in the United States, where more than two-thirds of the world's soybeans are grown, have caught on to the true value of soybeans in recent years. The health food craze and the rage for all things Asian have made *dòufǔ* a mainstay in supermarkets. It pleases the western palates and is just what the doctor ordered for the homesick Chinese.

ēn

grace, kindness

A person resting ☓ upon a square mat □ means to rely upon. It is combined with the heart ⺗ below. Whoever relies on his heart achieves grace.

Both *ēn* 恩 and *aì* 愛 use the image of the heart. The Chinese regard the heart as the place of highest human feelings and attributes. When the heart feels empathy for the oppressed, it has been touched by grace. A devoted couple, *ēnaìfūqī* 恩愛夫妻, cannot rely on love alone. It is grace and kindness that carry their relationship through.

fēng

shuǐ

geomancy, the art of placement

The wind, *fēng* 風, is a primal force of nature. It suggests movement through space. *Shuǐ* 水, the water, flows on timelessly, yielding to, but also shaping the land in its path.

Fēngshuǐ is the art of harmonizing man's relationship with his environment and the spirit world. This ancient science combines the eight trigrams which are patterns of lines representing the cosmos; the five elements of metal, wood, water, fire, and earth; and a large helping of astrology.

First appearing in the historical documents of Han, and later in the Jin dynasty, *fēngshuǐ* has evolved into a practice of deflecting bad luck so as to prevent personal failure and misfortune. This ancient philosophy has become very popular yet is still an ambiguity in the modern world.

As a study of time, space, and man, *fēngshuǐ* can also be applied to architectural planning to access health and vigor. As explained in *The Book of Rites*: "Do not change the way of heaven; do not obstruct the nature of the earth; do not disrupt the bonds between people." Surely, the Chinese were among the world's first environmentalists!

gōng

fū

kungfu

Work 工 and strength 力 produce *gōng* 功 . *Fū* 夫 shows an adult male standing in a distinguished pose.

Most people in the western world have seen *gōngfū* in Bruce Lee or Jackie Chan movies. What they do not realize is that there are two major schools of martial arts — Shaolin and Wudang.

Shaolin encourages superior swiftness and agility as exhibited in *gōngfū*. It was created by Buddhists as a form of defense and requires the external skills of speed and toughness.

Wudang motivates graceful inner-body exercises called *tàijí* 太極 or *tàijíquán* 太極拳 . Wudang sprang from the ancient Chinese religion of Taoism and stresses the internal skills of stillness and breathing.

With the development of modern weaponry, *gōngfū* is no longer used as a means of attacking or defending. Today it is simply a way of keeping fit. *Tàijí*, the soft and gentle art of shadow boxing, has in recent times become one of the most popular of the Chinese martial arts.

hóng

bāo

red envelope

Hóng 紅 names the family of red hues. *Bāo* 包 shows a baby in its mother's womb and signifies the wrapping up or holding of something.

Red symbolizes the vitality of life. In the past gold coins tied to red twine would be placed beneath the stove during the New Year holidays to represent "through brilliant fire comes abundant wealth." Only after the New Year's dinner would the coins be pulled out and handed to the children. It was hoped that the coins would expel evil and danger, and allow the children to put their pasts behind them so they could grow up strong and healthy.

It has only been in the last few decades that bright red envelopes containing money have become commonly used for occasions other than the New Year. Red envelopes have replaced gold lockets for a month-old baby, herbal medicines for a sick friend, and other traditional gifts for special events. The Chinese insist on the act of giving no matter how little one can give. After all, no amount of paper currency can ever outweigh the feelings in one's heart.

jià

qǔ

marry into, marry

A pig 豕 under a roof 宀 demonstrates the concept of home 家 . By adding a woman 女 to home, *jià* 嫁 takes the woman to a home. *Qǔ* 娶 figuratively means for a man to choose 取 a woman 女 .

The Chinese have a deep-seated faith in destiny. It is no wonder that so much time has been spent on worshipping powerful beings who control everything from the season's harvest to one's life partner.

Most Chinese believe that marriage is not just the joining of individuals, but a binding relationship between families. A person's feelings were secondary to the family's wishes. In the western world many people marry for love; but for the Chinese, the voices of tradition still whisper loudly in their ears.

Marriages are rarely prearranged today, but many marriages start off with some help from a local cupid — a matchmaker. In rural Taiwan, you can still find betrothal teas where nervous couples get their first glimpses of each other.

kuài

zi

chopsticks

Kuài 快 is a phonetic script that imitates the sound made by a pair of chopsticks. The upper image 𥫗 is added to denote the material, generally bamboo, that the chopsticks are made from. *Zi* 子 is used here as a noun suffix.

Chinese culinary culture is not just a matter of cooking techniques and fine food flavors, it also involves the etiquette of the tableware, the chopsticks. Chopsticks were used as early as the Shang dynasty and gained popularity over spoons in the fourteenth century. Japan and Korea not only borrowed the use of these eating utensils, they have recently integrated chopstick instructions into their elementary school curriculum.

A pair of chopsticks allows one to handle all kinds of Chinese food with perfect ease. Whether the food is as small as rice or as large as a whole fish, chopsticks can smoothly convey pieces to the mouth and still allow the diner to maintain a dignified posture.

The Moon 月 appears on the lower left, above it is the character for rising ㅗ , and on the right is a symbol that looks like a dragon's tail 㠯 . All together, we see the concept of a dragon soaring above the moon, bringing a transformation to the earth.

lóng

龍

dragon

In China *lóng* 龍 represents the spirit of the water, and is said to determine the shape of the landscape. A five-clawed dragon was once the emblem of imperial power and its use by commoners was forbidden. The tradition of the dragon as a symbol of authority, wealth, and respect still persists today.

It is considered a great honor to be born under the sign of the dragon. The belief is so strong that when the Year of the Dragon comes around, birth rates go up in the Chinese community. So many more children are born during the Year of the Dragon that classrooms become more crowded resulting in added competition. In Taiwan alone, an increase of 3 births per thousand occurred in 1976 and 1988. Imagine what might happen in the year 2000!

má

jìang

mahjongg

Má 麻 stands for flax and *jìang* 將 is the character for a general. There is only speculation as to where *májìang* got its name, no real documentation has been recorded.

During the Song dynasty *májìang* began as a game with 40 playing tiles. Today *májìang* uses 144 tiles. Four players each hold 16 tiles. Players give away what they do not want while trying not to give a tile that will help the opponents. It is like playing poker, bridge, and dominos simultaneously!

This game of wits and luck has been played by Chinese of all ages for over a hundred years. It offers mental relaxation and the excitement of healthy competition. Although not as widespread as *gōngfū*, *májìang* is gaining popularity in the western world.

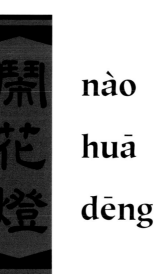

nào

huā

dēng

lantern parade

Nào 鬧 means to make joyful noises, *huā* 花 is the common term for flowers, and *dēng* 燈 is a lamp.

The Chinese celebrate the New Year according to the lunar calendar. The date falls between the end of January and early February in the western calendar. Traditionally, Chinese New Year festivities last for 15 days. On the last day of the Chinese New Year jubilee there is a lantern parade. During the parade the streets are filled with a procession of clowns, stilt walkers, lion dancers, performers in colorful costumes, and hundreds of lanterns. The display of a wide variety of lanterns is the climax of the New Year celebration.

During the Lantern Festival families come together to eat sweet rice balls. This traditional New Year dish is believed to bring good luck. After dinner people happily set out towards the town square where many beautiful lanterns are hung. Riddles are placed near the lanterns, and whoever is the first to figure one out receives a prize. After a night of fun and frolic, the new year officially begins.

ǒu

lotus seed

The topmost image ⁺⁺ is a pictograph of grass. On the left is an ancient plow 耒 mainly used to indicate farming. On the right is a phonetic script 禺 that gives the word a sound.

The lotus is an aquatic plant native to southern Asia and Australia. It is regarded as the supreme flower of summer. Its pale blossoms grace the tranquil lakes and pools of many Chinese parks and gardens. Under the influence of Buddhism, Chinese poets have praised the cleanliness and purity of the lotus flower rising above the muddy water. Unlike its water lily cousins which float on the water, lotus flowers and leaves can rise three to six feet above the water.

The Chinese make great use of every part of this special plant. The seeds are made into a sweet paste for desserts; the seed pods and stamens are used for medicine; and the roots, *ǒu* 藕, are canned or cooked as delicacies. The natural silky fibers inside the roots inspired an old Chinese saying, *ǒuduànsīlián* 藕斷絲連, which describes two lovers going their separate ways, yet the ties between them remain unbroken.

琵 **pí**

琶 **pā**

pipa

The top part of each word 珏 illustrates the shape of the tuning mechanism. The bottom parts 比 巴 are phonetic scripts to help sound out the words.

Of the many types of Chinese instrumental music, the art of plucking a lute called a *pípā* 琵琶 has thrived into the 20th century. It became highly popular during the Tang dynasty after it was brought to China by traders along the Silk Route. Only minor modifications have been made to the instrument over the years, and today it is held vertically when played.

A *pípā* can be used solo or in ensembles. It has the ability to produce sounds which express mood extremes. It can be tender and elegant one moment, but sharp and overzealous the next. For the romantic Chinese, *pípā* mirrors American's blues guitar. It is truly one jazzy instrument!

qí

páo

chipao

Qí 旗 literally means banner. *Páo* 袍 is a robe of any kind.

Qípáo evolved from the Manchurian style of military uniform in the Qing dynasty. When the Qing dynasty was overthrown and the Chinese Republic was formed, the military uniform of the "bannermen" lived on as formal wear for Chinese women. They wore a long blue gown with a high collar and a hemline between the knees and ankles.

As influence flowed in from the west, *qípáo* underwent its greatest transformation during the 1940's. Today new and improved variations that are no longer waist-huggingly tight result in an ease of movement. *Qípáo* is worn because of a sentimental longing for that dignified, graceful age in the history of Chinese fashion.

rěn

patience

A knife 刀 pointing ﹨ over the heart ⺗ is the ultimate state of patience.

Chinese people are often reminded of the saying, "There is a knife in the word *rěn* 忍 ." When one lives on the cutting edge, care and endurance are called for. The true meaning of patience is a firm and tolerant heart. As the sages advise, "When you are at the end of your patience, be patient."

Throughout the history of China, this philosophy has helped the people survive occupation and invasion by foreign forces. It took a collective effort of perseverance to come out of centuries of turmoil and achieve a prominent place in the world today.

shí

èr

shēng

xìao

Chinese Horoscope

Shí 十 is ten, *èr* 二 is two, *shēng* 生 means life, and *xìao* 肖 means animal.

Horoscope animals are not the exclusive property of the Chinese. Such totem year gods have been found in Egypt, Babylon, and Africa with notable similarities. The twelve animals in Chinese astrology are more than general signposts of the year, and more than the harbingers of the possible good or bad times ahead. They are considered to be a reflection of the universe itself.

A person's Chinese animal sign is as fundamental as his name, gender, and place of birth. One is tempted to flip through the lunar almanac to choose the right date and time to plan special occasions in order to avoid clashes with other signs. Although not all Chinese believe in the fabulous powers attributed to the Chinese horoscope, when each new year comes around modern Chinese still heartily greet it for the promises the new year holds.

tú

zhāng

chop, seal

Tú 圖 means picture and *zhāng* 章 means chop.

A *túzhāng*, which is also known as a chop, is a stamp of a person's name. The chop is usually carved by hand and made of bamboo, wood, or fine stone. The chop is dipped in red paste and used for the signing of important papers. Seals and chops have been widely used since the Zhou dynasty. Not only can they authenticate documents, official or private, they also function aesthetically for the cultural elite of China. Whereas people today wear brand-name clothing to indicate wealth and class, older Chinese measure a person's status by glancing at his seal.

Today a seal enables a person to be in two places at the same time. It can sign important papers when one cannot be present. It is a sign of good faith, sometimes more acceptable than one's own signature. You cannot complete a procedure unless you put your chop on the paper, be it a contract, legal paper, bank transaction, or even a marriage certificate.

wǒ

我

I, me

This pictograph depicts an ax-like weapon 戈 along with a long-shafted tool 手. The word *wǒ* 我 was used to indicate the first person.

The image of a capital "I" does not exist in Chinese culture. Individualism is associated with a lack of sympathy, selfishness, and greed by the Chinese.

According to Zhuang Zi, one must have "no self" and "no fame" in order to abide with the nature of things. An emphasis on conforming to the group and maintaining harmony is always held in high regard. An act of disagreement is considered an act of disrespect, and the showing of one's superior ability is equated with excessive pride. Assertiveness is discouraged throughout the course of one's life, and humility is encouraged.

xìao

shùn

filial piety

Xìao 孝 shows an old man 耂 supported by his son 子; and *shùn* 順 represents obedience, loyalty, and devotion to parents.

Confucius, the famous Chinese philosopher, believed that since strong family ties formed the basis of a stable society, family relationships should be governed by mutual respect, as in the bond of respect between parents and children.

Since parents do their very best to raise their children, the children are expected to be completely obedient in return. A centuries-old Chinese saying, "No parents in the world can be wrong," illustrates belief in total respect towards adults. As China becomes less isolated, Chinese parents allow their children more freedom of expression; but the basic idea of pleasing one's parents, even after they pass away, has been engraved in the mind of almost every Chinese.

Yù 玉 resembles a string of three jade pieces. The point 丶 was a late addition in order to distinguish *yù* from *wáng* 王 which means king.

yù

jade

Jade, a semiprecious stone, has been treasured by the Chinese more than any other natural material. The classic jade of China is known as nephrite. Because of its smoothness and elegant coloring, jade has been celebrated in the life of the Chinese for millennia. As early as the Xia dynasty, jade symbolized human virtues because of its durability, rarity, and beauty. Social laws and institutions were preserved in jade emblems, and it was of utmost importance in religious rites.

Carved jade is more refined today. Its mastery challenges not only the skill but also the imagination of the artist. To make a fine carving, jade is polished with abrasive sand and water. Without a doubt, the fact that Chinese students often excel in school comes from the belief, "Jade which is not chiseled and polished cannot become an article of beauty."

中
國

zhōng

guó

China

Visually, *Zhōng* 中 shows a flagpole planted in a circle to mean center or middle. *Guó* 國 is composed of three main parts: mouth 口 for people, spear 戈 for defense, and the symbol 口 for boundary. *Guó* is the perfect character to signify a country, state, or nation.

For centuries the Chinese people have considered their country to be the center of the universe. They were self-sufficient and developed a unique culture that influenced their neighbors.

Within the People's Republic of China today, 94% of the population is of Han descent. The remaining 70 million people are composed of 55 minority groups. Throughout the history of China these minorities have maintained their own way of life. In modern times minority children study their own ethnic languages as well as Chinese in school.

Although China is not a rich country, it is developing rapidly. Today China is striving to hold on to its tradition and timeless wisdom. At the same time the world's oldest surviving civilization forges ahead eagerly into the 21st century.

Tones

Every Chinese character has a specific tone when spoken in Mandarin. Changing the tone changes the meaning of the word.

The five basic tones are:

ˉ Continuous Tone... similar to the reciting of "A, B, C, D..."
ˊ Rising Tone .... similar to a surprised "Huh?"
ˇ Drawling Tone....... similar to an indecisive "Well..."
ˋ Falling Tone.......... similar to a purposeful "Yes!"
Neutral Tone .... similar to a soft and short "Mama..."

Sounds

Vowels:

Mandarin has 6 simple vowels:

a as in mama
e as in learn or get (when preceded by i or u)
i as in sit or sir (when preceded by zh, ch, sh, or r)
o as in drop or grow (when followed by ng)
u as in look
ü similar to the French u in *rue*

Mandarin has 15 compound vowels:

ai as in lie
ao as in how
ei as in clay
ou as in low
ui as in way
iao as in meow
and *ia, ie, iu, ua, un, uo, üa, üe,* and, *uai*

Consonants:

There are 24 consonants in Mandarin. Most of them are very much like the consonants in English except for the following:

c	its (strongly aspirated)	*x*	she
ch	children	*y*	yet
j	jeep	*z*	plants (without aspiration)
q	cheek	*zh*	sludge
sh	shore		

Timeline of Chinese History

Xia (2300-1650BC) ➡ **Shang** (1650-1027BC) ➡ **Zhou** (1027-221BC) ➡ Warring States (481-221BC) ➡ Qin (221-207BC) ➡ **Han** (207BC-220AD) ➡ Period of the Three Kingdoms (220-280AD) ➡ **Jin** (265-420AD) ➡ Northern & Southern Dynasties (301-589AD) ➡ Sui (589-618AD) ➡ **Tang** (618-907AD) ➡ Five Dynasties & Ten Kingdoms (907-960AD) ➡ **Song** (960-1279AD) ➡ Yuan (1279-1368AD) ➡ Ming (1368-1644AD) ➡ **Qing** (1644-1912AD) ➡ **Chinese Republic** (1912-1949AD) ➡ Split of **Mainland** & **Taiwan** (1949-today)

(Periods in bold face were mentioned in the book.)